This is a picture of life and death.

The body is depicted as a red diamond, growing from the point of birth and then contracting in old age—but even as the body contracts, wisdom and spirit continue to grow until they reach the rainbow at the top of the drawing.

We just grow over the rainbow. Graduate, from life into death.

— Helen Ansley

Life's Finishing School: What Next?

A Ninety-Year-Old's View of Death and Dying a Good Death

See Reverse Side of the Book for A Ninety-Year-Old's View of Life and Living a Good Life

by

Helen Green Ansley

Illustrations by Marion Weber

**Conscious Living / Conscious Dying:
A Project of the Institute of Noetic Sciences**

I see life as a Finishing School, the Ultimate Finishing School, with a full curriculum that teaches us Conscious Living, so that we may graduate—with honors—with a Conscious Death.

—Helen Ansley

For permission to reprint portions of this work contact
Institute of Noetic Sciences
475 Gate Five Road, Suite 300
Box 909
Sausalito, CA 94966-0909
(415) 331-5650

Produced for the Institute of Noetic Sciences
by Carol Guion
with the help of Sharon Skolnick and Lisa Mertz

Cover design: Carol Guion
Charts design: Helen Ansley
Cover and charts production art: Sharon Skolnick

Special thanks to Noel Andrews, Violet Cleveland,
Laura Franklin and Stephen Jamison for their contributions

Printed by United Graphics of Indiana, Inc., Terre Haute

ISBN 0-943951-01-1

Price $7.50
$6.60 to members of the Institute of Noetic Sciences

Any additional gifts will go directly to the Institute's
Conscious Living/Conscious Dying Project,
and are tax-deductible.

Contents

Life's Finishing School: What Next?
A Ninety-Year-Old's View
of Death and Dying
a Good Death

See reverse side of the book for
Life's Finishing School: What Now?
A Ninety-Year-Old's View
of Life and Living
a Good Life

Introduction

by John White

Death—the great unknown, the final frontier. That is the view of my friend Helen Ansley, now 90 years old. She helped a group of us explore this frontier when she gave a talk entitled "What's Wrong with Dying?" Advocating euthanasia as a means of preserving a person's dignity and financial condition, she stated that it is both ethical and humane to allow a person to choose the time and manner of death. It is that for the person *and* for his or her survivors.

Helen Ansley contends that one should realistically face the inevitable, not morbidly, but creatively. "Why not view death as a celebration?" she suggests. "Does it really have to be slow and painful and sad? Is it really so bad? I doubt it. We have birthdays—why not deathdays?"

Her joyful and creative approach to the last stage of life is why I wrote about her in "Appendix 4" of my book *A Practical Guide to Death and Dying*. Helen's approach should cause us all to reflect on the quality of our lives and what "dying a good death" can mean for that.

Foreword

by Paul Brenner, MD

At a conference of the American Holistic Medical Association I gravitated towards a small animated group of physicians surrounding an elderly gray-haired woman whose lively gesticulation, humor, and obvious joy of life kept everyone on their toes. After each statement the docs would nudge each other and whisper, "Hell of a woman, hell of a woman."

I too was drawn to this most exciting person whom I now fondly call "Toots" but is better known as Helen Ansley. Helen is 90 years old and a major spokesperson for conscious living, conscious dying.

"If you have lived to 85 or 90, what do you do with the rest of your life? It is time to talk about what possibilities exist for a good death and how we can take control over where, how, and when we die," she says.

Helen Ansley is not ready to die yet—she has people to talk to, people to awaken. She is not the prophet of death, but rather the prophet of life, realism, and beauty. Here are some of her outrageous—and sensible—solutions. Enjoy and ponder.

A Note From The Illustrator

by Marion Weber

It is my sincere hope that these illustrations will help stimulate *your* imagination and *your* visions around dying well and living well.

We are all artists blessed with awesome imaginations. The only things holding us back are fear and judgment.

So let these two feelings go and breathe in playfulness, trust, spontaneity and a spirit of adventure. And see what emerges!

Here is a list of what's needed in order to explore with your imagination:

1. one hour
2. a space that feels safe and comfortable
3. willingness
4. openness
5. relaxed body
6. music
7. tools (paper, pencils, etc.)

Begin by closing your eyes. Feel your body completely held by the Earth. Visualize spirit energy like a gentle cape resting on your head, shoulders and arms. Visualize a warm protective circle around you. Feel your pulse in your hands.

Now pick up a pencil and with your eyes still closed let your hand move spontaneously across the paper, trusting your own rhythm. Open your eyes. See if the lines suggest anything to you.

Now with the same totally relaxed free manner open your imagination concerning some subject, some aspect of life or death. Sit with that subject, open to receiving an image about it. When the image comes, lovingly draw it. There is no right way to draw it. There is no wrong way to draw it. Only your way.

Be surprised!
Have fun!
Enjoy your beautiful imagination.
It is a gift!
Share it with a friend!

Artist Marion Weber is on the Board of Directors of the Institute of Noetic Sciences, and on the Steering Committee of its Conscious Living / Conscious Dying Project.

Tony Basilio is on the Steering Committee of our Institute of Noetic Sciences' Conscious Living / Conscious Dying Project. Here is a poem he wrote for one of our meetings:

Seeds Are The Ticket To Ride

I think we would all do well,
to get quiet and *listen* better . . .
We're too ready to *do*.
Too much *do* and not enough *listen*.
We misuse the mind.

We create fear and greed, worry, apprehension,
. . . then believe it,
then project *that* on the screen,
then attack the screen!

. . . Better to change the film . . .
Our mind. Thoughts. Beliefs.

There's nothing wrong with the world.
Our perceptions need to be healed.
We think we live a life
We think there's somebody who lives a life . . .
there *isn't*.

Life lives itself. One Life living. We get to experience it.

They give you a body when you come *into* life.
We think life *is* the body.
It isn't.
The body's just the ticket to ride.

It's the vehicle.
Life was there before the body,
and will be after.
Bodies come and go,
Life is infinite.

When you ride a car across the land . . .
the car *isn't* the land . . .
it's the vehicle *through* the land.

When you ride a body through life . . .
the body *isn't* the life,
it's the vehicle, *through* the life.

We've got the *vehicle* confused with the *life*.
And this is the basis of many seeming problems.
Life Lives.

It's an ongoing continuum. Bodies come in.
Bodies go out.

Life doesn't die.
Vehicles die.
Bodies die.
Bodies come in.
Bodies go out.
Life Lives.

You are not the body.
The body is the container for what you are,
while you're here.

When the container goes,
your membership in life
just takes another form.
Life absorbs the living back unto itself,
and spits off dead bodies.

You don't need a body to be among the living.
Your very *essence is* the living.
Timeless. Infinite. Perfect.
Undying. Unchanging. Beyond Cause.
God.

That is the One Life that Lives.
The body is a seed of God.

Seeds come.
Seeds sprout.
Seeds flower,
Seeds die.
More seeds come.

Seeds are the tickets to ride.
There's one life behind them all.
One Life, that the seeds grant us *entry to.*
Seeds are the vehicles, *into* and *through* life.
Body seeds. They're like Passports . . .
Entry visas.

We came in and out of life before,
We come in and out of life again . . .
Loop-de-loops on the roller-coaster,
into the tunnel, through the tunnel,
out of the tunnel.
Reincarnation?
. . . O.K.
One Life Living.
Lotsa different little tickets in and out.
One Life Living
All of us.

Who *lives* a life?
What is *a* life?
but an initiation . . . into Forever.
A Rite of Passage . . . into Existence, A Birth.
A Life . . . is a Birth.
A Death . . . is the *end* of a Birth!

Basic Training. Preparation.
FOR WHO YOU REALLY ARE.

And we only complete a life when we've lived through a death;
and we live through a death, by knowing there *is* no death.
What we really are can't die.
IT ALWAYS WAS.
We're not a body

WHAT ALWAYS WAS WILL ALWAYS BE.
Bodies come and go.
And things that come and go . . . will pass.

Life's Finishing School:
A Curriculum
for Dying Well

". . . so few know the art of dying. For dying, like living, is an art and if only most of us mastered the art of dying as much as we seek to master the art of living, there would be many more happy deaths.

"The fact of the matter, however, is that the art of living is not different from the art of dying; in fact, the one flows into the other, and cannot be separated one from the other. [S]He who has mastered the art of living has already mastered the art of dying; to each, death holds no terrors."

—M. V. Kamath

Dying: Everybody Does It, But Nobody Talks About It

All my life, as I grew older and entered a different stage of life, there was always a new challenge and something new to learn. At 90 I think I've done everything I'm supposed to do. I have more time now and I'm free to explore new ways to look at things, and try to figure out what comes next.

I think my final task is finding a good way, a good place, to die, because that's what comes next for me—and it's something that needs to be done better!

Death is a subject that continues to be taboo in our society. More often than not it is ignored as something too painful to contemplate and denied as long as possible. By the time we get around to dying, it's too late to do anything constructive about it.

Death is the natural end of life on Earth—the final stage. No one would want to live forever. Why, then, in our culture, is it usually regarded as a tragedy, a failure of life, rather than an *achievement of death*?

At present there is no such thing as a good death. It's always regarded as a failure . . .

We plan ahead for—and celebrate—the other major events in our life—education, job, marriage, children, vacations, retirement. Lots of people even earn a living helping us plan for those events. Why don't we plan for and celebrate this final event?

Why can't we explore better ways of dying? Why don't we create suitable environments for a good death—a death with dignity?

We should learn how to take control of our own death. Make the arrangements, make peace with the people we must make peace with, finish our unfinished business and, when we're ready, let go and get on with it.

The exercise on the next page can help you see what you really want, and what you need to do to make this come to pass.

Picturing Your Ideal Death

Imagine that you can create how and when you are going to die. Picture your ideal death. Where are you? Who is with you? Or would you rather be alone? How are you feeling? Now look to see if there is anything in your present life that you might want to do to assure this ideal death. Are there relationships / legal matters / tidying up that need your attention?

I'd love to die some place where there's a view,
a place where you can see nature,
and God is there
and God is in you
and you're just getting together again.

Now is the time to relinquish our archaic and barbaric views of aging, dying, and death and to replace them with intelligent, creative and practical concepts.

I'm not telling people that life isn't worth living, because I know nothing more fascinating. I don't see death as the end of life, but only as a transformation, a continuum. Einstein knew energy could not be created or destroyed. We just keep going on.

I don't see death as the end of life, but only as transformation . . .

Our Last Right: Death with Dignity

Approximately 85% of the older people in the United States die in institutions of some kind. About 15% die in their own homes.

The older generation used to find a sense of purpose in the homes of their families, but this isn't the case anymore.

Society doesn't realize it, but the biggest fear the elderly have isn't death. It's winding up like a vegetable, unable to communicate, and costing survivors or taxpayers thousands of dollars.

It isn't, then, their life that's prolonged. It's their dying that's postponed. Old age should not be extended to the point where life becomes unbearable.

It seems to me we all ought to have choices about how we die. When death is imminent, there should be creative options available. If I get the feeling I'm ready to go, then I want to go.

But if you're in an institution it's going to cost you a lot, even if you only go there at the end of your life. I'm told that half of your total medical expenses throughout your life come within the last year or two of your life—and a lot of that within the last six to eight weeks. The government picks up the tab when our own funds run out. The government is paying to keep us from dying—and the government is us.

If you go to a hospital they do everything to keep you alive. You're put on machines, whether you want it or not. "Don't let them die" is the philosophy. The same is true of nursing homes, and if you get angry about it, and say you want to die, they give you something to cheer you up. All the medication does is cause confusion. Nobody, but nobody, will talk to you about how you can die!

I've known too many people whose families just won't talk to them about dying. Oh, they say, we want you here! Oh, you mustn't leave us!

It's usually the children who can't bear to part with their parents. The parents know when they're ready to go, and they wish people would quit trying to hang onto them.

A relative of mine was dying after a heart operation, I think it was his second one. The son said, "Dad, you mustn't leave us. You can't leave us now, we need you." His father came back to consciousness and said, "Don't ever do that to me again!" And that's what we do to people—we selfishly try to keep them around.

Our whole culture has said, get out of the way, get out of the way, you're a burden. Then your family says, you mustn't leave, you mustn't leave, you mustn't talk about dying. Just get out of the way, and here's the bill.

Some people just want to accept whatever comes and not do anything about it. Some people will fight every inch of the way, and if they have enough money, it's all right.

It might be that when life becomes just not worth living that you could get out of it, no matter what your age. But you should be the one to decide when.

But any attempt to plan for a good death for ourselves is considered a sign of deep depression, of mental illness, and we're liable to be turned over—by a well-meaning close relative—to the care of a psychiatrist, whose responsibility it is to return us to "normal" mental health and to prevent any suicide attempt.

I can't buy a gun, I don't take any prescription drugs, and to get anything that could help me die, I'd have to involve somebody else. In most states it is a crime to help anyone, regardless of age or quality of life, to plan their own death.

Society demands that the health professional prolong life, no matter what the cost. The Hemlock Society is working to change the laws in those states which won't even let doctors help their patients die peacefully.

If you have not made out a Living Will, this is the time to do it. See page 62 for where you can send for free forms. Then let your family and friends know you have it, that you have signed it, and tell them where you have put it.

But even having a Living Will is not enough—you must have someone who will fight for your right to die. Make out a Durable Power of Attorney for Health Care to give to one or two of your friends the legal power to be your advocate if you are not able to make your wishes known. Two are better in case one isn't near when needed. Just make sure they may act independently and not need to co-sign a decision.

Having a living will is not enough. You must have someone willing to fight for you . . .

A friend of mine who lived alone went to the hospital suddenly in the middle of the night, and they found a burst colon.

I knew she had signed a Living Will, but her family wouldn't ever talk to her about it. They kept her alive, because they had to have two doctors agree that death is imminent and nothing can be done, and the doctors wouldn't agree. They tried three different operations on her, at great expense and suffering, and finally at the end of four weeks they let her go.

I knew she wanted that from the beginning. It made me mad, so at that point I wrote:

I am more than Flesh and Blood and Sinew!
I am a PERSON, not a Doctor's Toy!
It's MY life to end or to continue!
It's MY life to suffer or enjoy!

I'm a person, not a doctor's toy . . .

Writing Your Will

Writing your will can be an "exercise in utility". You might just discover what your real treasures are, and with whom you'd like to leave them.

In the space below begin listing what you have to leave, and picture whom they should go to: your car, your cufflinks, your cat, perhaps.

What other assets should you list? What books or poems or pictures do you want your friends to have? What words that you haven't told them?

One gift we can give ourselves is the gift of forgiving others. Here is a wonderful exercise:

Expansion

Close your eyes and picture your heart as a beautiful glowing ball. Take whatever time you need to really see this (or feel—some people don't "see"). What color is it? Picture—or feel—this light expanding through your entire body. Now let it seep out around your body. Now it's growing out into the room, and through the walls, and out into the street and through the neighborhood and the city and the county and the state and the country and the continent and the world and the universe. Now let it come back in again.

If I were given just one wish
I know what it would be for.
I'd simply wish that I could have
A hundred wishes more!

This was my first poem, written a long time ago. Since then, I have written many poems—to express both joy and pain.

As the century and I went into the 70s I began an active study of conscious dying. My study was quickened by the dying and death of my husband Frank in 1974.

When my husband was dying I wrote

We're not afraid of death, but why must dying
Be so drawn out, so hard for those who care?
Why do you all insist we keep on trying to live,
When life is almost more than we can bear?

Why can't you let us go with smiling faces,
Knowing that what we want is for the best,
And knowing well that were you in our places,
You would be longing, too, for peace and rest?

We've had our share of happiness and sorrow,
We've had a good life and our work is done.
Why must we face tomorrow—and tomorrow—
When all the things we've known and loved
—Are gone?

Late May, 1974:

Why not conceive of death as Re-creation,
A time of pain and *joy—as at the time of birth?*
Why not give us a Deathday celebration
For our new life beyond this life on Earth?

Why not conceive of death as Re-creation . . .
Why not a Deathday celebration?

After my husband died in July, I visited old friends in Canada, and wrote in their guest book:

While Frank was dying
I thought about Death
And what could be done about it.
Does it have to be slow and painful and sad?
Is it really so bad? I doubt it.

I've also been thinking a lot about Life
And how, on this Earth, to renew it;
And I know that this time
In this place
With these friends
Is the very best way I could do it!

A year after my husband's death I decided to move up to Bellevue, Washington, where my older son lived, and I wrote:

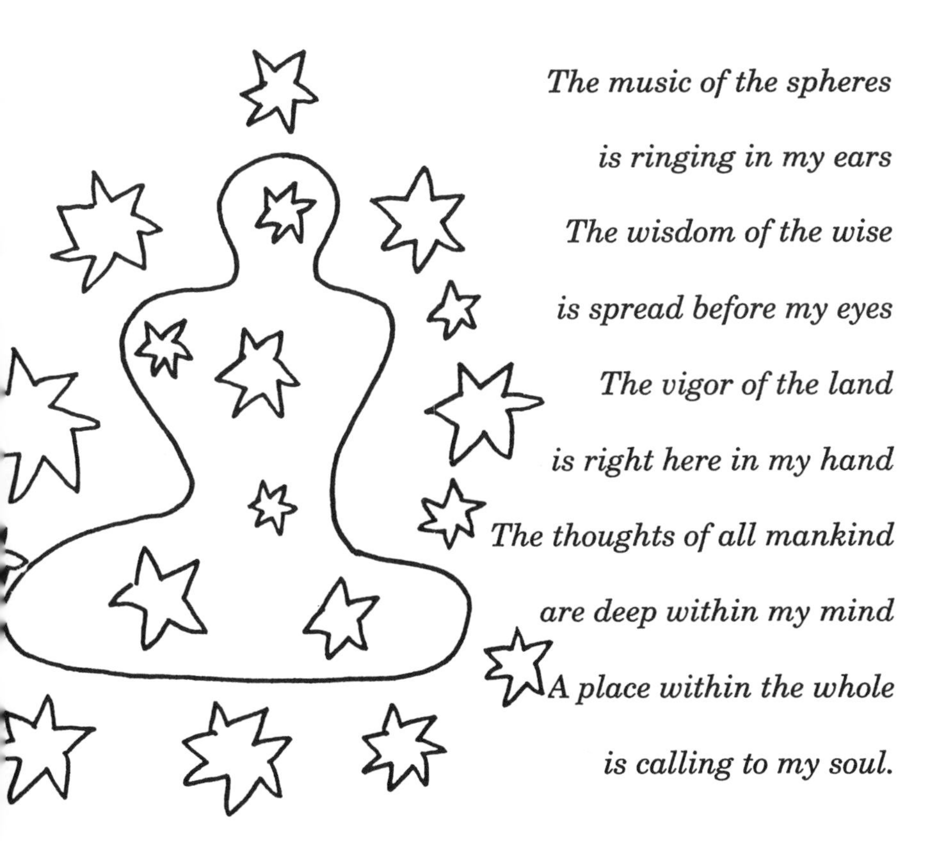

The music of the spheres

is ringing in my ears

The wisdom of the wise

is spread before my eyes

The vigor of the land

is right here in my hand

The thoughts of all mankind

are deep within my mind

A place within the whole

is calling to my soul.

As I watched two of my friends being kept alive for months against their wishes, I had to make some humor out of it—or cry my heart out.

Why Not Die Laughing?

The High Cost of Living
Is merely a joke—
It's the High Cost of Dying
That's keeping us broke!
The Doctors and Lawyers
Must all have their share
And those horrible prices
For Nursing Home Care!
The Law won't permit
Any person to kill us—
But any and all
Are encouraged to bill us!

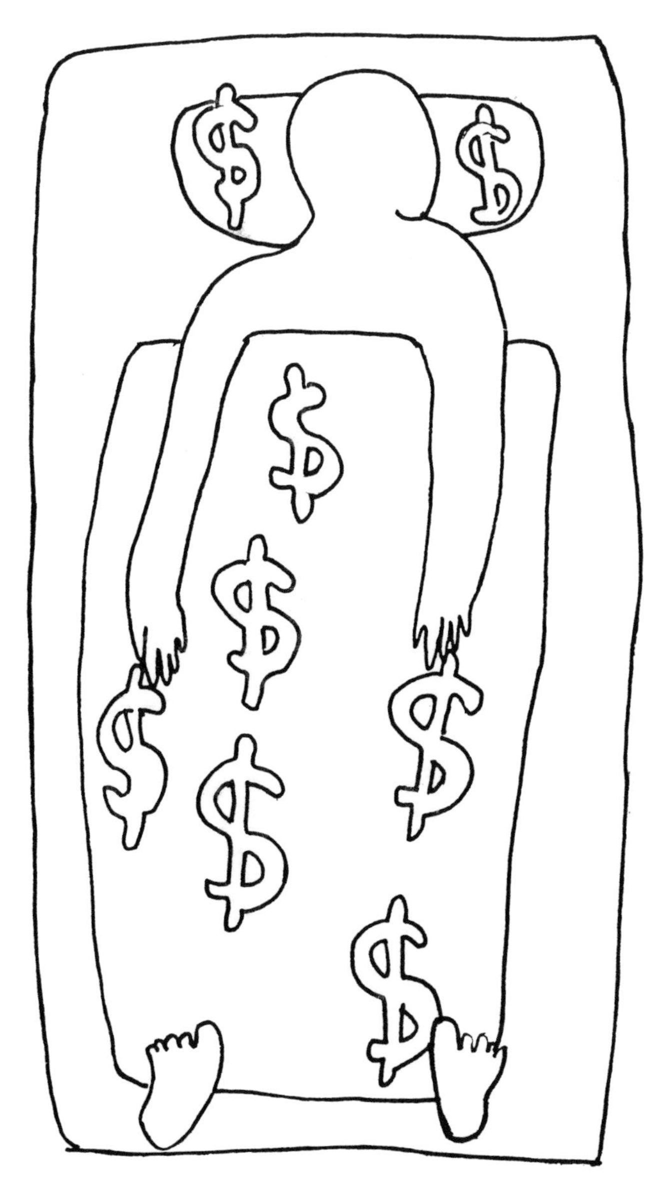

It's the high cost of dying that's keeping us broke!

Dr. Brenner and I . . .

And then Dr. Paul Brenner got me down to Carmel to give a talk at a church, and I had to announce it at the morning service. So I marched up to the platform and said

Dr. Paul Brenner and I
Are searching for GOOD ways to die.
I think we can do it
If we put our minds to it.
You never can tell till you try!

The following pages will give you an idea of what I've been saying in talks since then. It is never twice alike—it always depends on the time allowed and on the audience.

The Ultimate Finishing School

I want a place that you could call The Ultimate Finishing School. Here you go to learn to die in style, your own style. And there are different styles of dying.

What I want is to do research with people into *conscious* dying. We can explore our thoughts on death in the same spirit we would explore any new frontier—experiencing the process as it goes along, not denying its presence.

We will hold classes, to learn, to experiment in different ways of meditating, for example. We'll explore stuff that isn't even in any of the books yet. Most importantly, we'll be exploring our own feelings about death and what we can do about it.

Dag Hammerskjold said, "You have not done enough, you have never done enough, so long as it is still possible that you have something of value to contribute." It might even be that people would come to this Ultimate Finishing School and learn that they still had something to contribute.

We'll attract the people who still have something to give, their own thoughts about dying, their own thoughts about life, death, life after death even. I don't think I want to come back to this Earth—I think I'd like to go to another planet, if you don't mind. But if somebody wants to come back, ok, but there ought to be different things to talk about, freely.

We'll continue studying, continue exploring, so it's a real finishing school. There are different styles of death, just as there are different styles of living—from being accepting, sensual, humorous, to being tragic, defiant, or in quest of life's next chapter. We'll study the different styles of life, and discover what style we belong to, and then plan a proper death.

Churches could help by creating homes for elderly people who no longer have a place to live. Not a church institution, but just a family —three to ten people—enough so you can have a game of bridge or go out—you could hire a taxi together.

We want to be doing something, by our very dying we would be helping, would be giving something in dying.

You know, back in 1973 I spent three dollars for a horoscope. It told me I would develop an interest in death, and even my death might have some unusual publicity. Perhaps I can be useful after all—even at 90.

Hopefully, we keep growing and growing into the cosmos—a beautiful rainbow of death, and whatever comes next. We graduate from this stage, if we have learned enough—without even being ill!

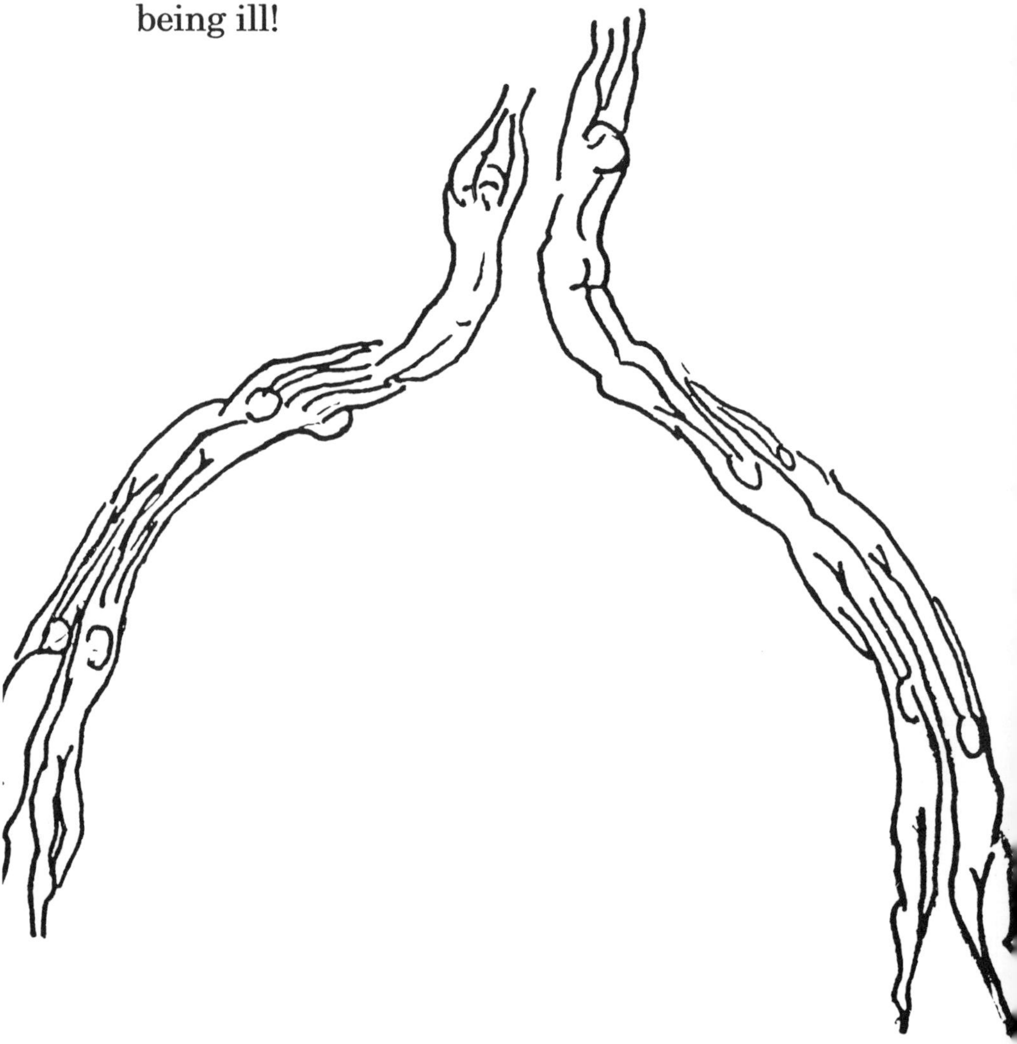

A beautiful rainbow of death, and whatever comes next . . .

Appreciation

Make a list here of people who have been important in your life. Think about why. Try to put it into words. Have you told them this?

WAY OUT INN

The Way Out Inn

So now I want to establish a place where other people can explore dying with me and where I can die—a Way Out Inn. I've known enough people who seemed to die when they were ready. This could be the place where we *could* get ready, where we could prepare for the next great adventure.

For example, the Way Out Inn could be a place to spend our last week or ten days making our own funeral arrangements, saying goodbye to friends, giving away our remaining treasures when we're sure we no longer need them.

But now there's no place for a final celebration of a good life, surrounded by a few people who would rejoice with you in the achievement of a good death, at an appropriate time, in a peaceful manner, without the huge expense of an intensive-care death in a hospital or a long drawn-out decline in a nursing home.

For myself I'd like to be in a simple place either in the woods or with a wide view.

LAST RESORT

A Last Resort

I wish there were a place for gracious dying

A high place with a distant view

where we could gather for a celebration

of life

and death

and friendships, old and new.

I'd like a place where there would be good music,

good food and wine and laughter,

games and fun

and time for quiet talk with friends,

and good discussion of what will happen

when this life is done.

• Can't we have a place where mentally alert people can plan to go when they're ready to die? Some smart business person could make a lot of money out of a "last resort" like that.

• I want to use up my money before I die, at a wonderful Last Resort. This is one way people can choose to die.

• We could have a celebration of death with our friends, with songs and laughter.

• We could choose to leave in an altered state of consciousness, such as leaving the body through meditation or fasting, or anything that can get you out of your body so you can stay there.

• We could explore gentle ways of dying—holding hands, breathing, relaxing, letting go. We could die with our minds, without taking any drugs, without involving anybody in killing us.

• Webster defines suicide as the act or an instance of taking one's own life voluntarily and intentionally, especially by a person of years of discretion and of sound mind. Surely this is one way out we will explore.

• "Death Takes a Holiday": I have a fantasy of like-minded people taking a final holiday. We could spend all our money on a wonderful final bash, on a cruise ship, say. Sail off into the sunset, literally, and die having a good time.

• You know, I want someone who'll say to me, "It's all right, Helen. You did a good job. You can go now."

One of the remarkable things about saintly people is that even their deaths are often acts of inspiration and love . . .

"We learn so much by example, by simply observing others and then trying to model our behavior after theirs. Inspiration begets imitation—a perfectly valid way to educate, and especially so with regard to death, when used consciously. That is because our fear of dying is, to a large extent, unconscious imitation. Part of our fear of dying is due to nothing more than modeling of widespread social behavior.

"In 1963 an extraordinary East Indian spiritual teacher named Govindananda died at age 137. He had lived an incredibly strenuous life, actually journeying around the world by foot. Many heads of state were his friends, yet he lived humbly in a small jungle hut. When he became aware that it was time to die, he spoke quietly to a few disciples with him, gave a final blessing—'Live right life, worship God'—lay down, rested his head on his right palm in his usual sleeping position, and simply stopped breathing.

"One of the remarkable things about saintly people is that even their deaths are often acts of inspiration and love. Mahatma Gandhi trained himself well enough to have the name of God on his lips at the moment of death; Joan of Arc died saying the name of Christ."

—John White

Reprinted with permission from Chapter 11 of A Practical Guide to Death and Dying *(Quest Books, 1988) ©1980, 1988 John White*

What Next?

Make a list here of the things that have given you feelings of joy or satisfaction.

Now sum all this up into

Your Epitaph:

If after you die there is to be a gravemarker, or a plaque somewhere, or perhaps a memoriam in a book frontispiece: What would it say?

Now go back to your list of things that have given you feelings of joy. Are there still things that you hope to accomplish? So close the book now and go and do them.

Some of My Favorite Books About: Death with Dignity

• *To Die with Style*, by Marjorie McCoy (Abington Press, 1974). I met Marjorie when I heard her describe her book back in 1974, and we became friends. She describes six styles, so you can identify the style you want. One is *The Accepting Style*: For everything there is a season. An accepting lifestyle meets death as an inevitable part of creation. You don't want to keep on living. Death becomes a goal, a fulfillment. *Do Not Go Gentle Into That Good Night* is a defiant lifestyle that rebels against death, a personal destroyer. Then there's a *Sensual Lifestyle*: Eat drink and be merry for tomorrow we die . . . that fears death as a denial of human being. And then: *No One Ever Died With Warm Feet*: a humorous lifestyle that dances with death around the edges of ultimate mystery. Or *Good Night Sweet Prince*, a tragic lifestyle that experiences death as always too soon. If you want to feel tragic—oh, poor me, I'm dying—ok, we'll let you die in that style, help you do it that way, but my style is—*Come Now, Greatest Of Feasts*, a questing lifestyle that seeks to find in death the meaning of existence.

• *Last Rights: A Case for the Good Death*, by Marya Mannes (William Morrow and Co., 1973). This started me reading on the subject.

• *Letting Go*, by Richard Boerstler (Associates in Thanatology, 1985)—a beautifully helpful book by a truly gentle person.

• *Common Sense Suicide: The Final Right*, by Doris Portwood (Dodd, Mead, 1978). This makes a lot of sense to me! It's a practical book.

• *Suicide After Sixty: The Final Alternative*, by Marv Miller (Springer Series on Death and Suicide, 1979).

• *Between Life and Death*, by Robert Kastenbaum (Springer, 1979).

• *A Practical Guide to Death and Dying: How to Conquer Your Fear and Anxiety*, by John White (Quest Books, 1988). Planning ahead—putting your house in order ahead of time, so others won't mess things up afterwards. Of course I like this book, especially since I'm Appendix 4 in the 1988 edition.

• *Let Me Die Before I Wake: Hemlock's Book of Self-Deliverance*, by Derek Humphrey (Hemlock Society, 1983). This even includes lethal amounts of drugs you can use.

• *Heading Toward Omega: In Search of the Meaning of the Near-Death Experience*, by Kenneth Ring (William Morrow and Co., 1984).

The After-Death Experience

• *Journeys Out of the Body*, by Robert Monroe (Doubleday, 1971). He talked to our SAGE group in 1973. When I heard him talk about journeys out of the body, I *knew* it was true.

• *Far Journeys*, by Robert Monroe (Doubleday, 1985).

• *The Nature of Personal Reality: A Seth Book*, by Jane Roberts (Prentice Hall, 1974). I liked this the best of Jane Roberts' books.

• *The After-Death Journal of an American Philosopher: The World View of William James*, by Jane Roberts (Prentice Hall, 1978). I particularly enjoyed this one. It made a lot of sense.

• *Breakthrough to Creativity*, by Shafica Karagulla (DeVorss, 1974). I knew the congressman she mentioned. I *knew* what she wrote was true.

• *Through the Curtain*, by Shafica Karagulla with Viola Neal (DeVorss, 1983).

• *From My World to Yours*, by Jasper Swain (Walker and Co., 1977).

• *Life Never Ends*, by Kay Leedy (Coleman Graphics, 1983). She received and then gave me very real answers to my questions.

• *Aliens Among Us*, by Ruth Montgomery (Putnam, 1985).

Celebration of Life

• *Celebration of Life*, by Norman Cousins (1974).

• *Human Options*, by Norman Cousins (1981).

• *Head First*, by Norman Cousins (1989).

• *Your Second Life: The SAGE Experience*, by Gay Luce (Delacorte Press, 1979).

• *Health is a Question of Balance*, by Paul Brenner (DeVorss, 1978).

• *Higher Creativity*, by Willis Harman (Tarcher, 1984).

• *Healthful Aging*, by Geri Burdman (Prentice Hall, 1986).

• *Alternative Health Guide*, by Brian Inglis and Ruth West (Alfred Knopf, 1983).

• *A Good Age*, by Alex Comfort (Crown, 1976).

• *Age Wave*, by Ken Dychtwald (Tarcher, 1989).

• *BodyMind*, by Ken Dychtwald (Tarcher, 1977).

All but two (whom I haven't met) of these authors are friends of mine. I know and feel deeply the truth of what they write. They and their books have greatly influenced my life, from 1974 to the present. They gave me courage to speak out and be different.

The Creative Process: Suggested by Marion Weber

• *Drawing on the Artist Within*, by Betty Edwards (Simon and Schuster, 1987).

• *Drawing on the Right Side of the Brain*, by Betty Edwards (J. P. Tarcher, Inc., 1979).

- *Illuminations—The Healing Image*, by Madeline McMurray (Wingbow Press, 1988).

- *Drawing the Light From Within*, by Judith Cornell (Prentice Hall, 1990).

- *Creative Visualization*, by Shakti Gawain (New World Library, 1978).

- *Living with Vision*, by Linda Marks (Knowledge Systems, Inc., 1989).

- *On Not Being Able to Paint*, by Joanna Field (J. P. Tarcher, Inc., 1957).

- *Seeing with the Mind's Eye*, by Mike Samuels and Nancy Samuels (Random House, 1975).

- *The Power of Your Other Hand*, by Lucia Capachione (New Castle Publishing, 1988).

For an extensive bibliography, write to
the Conscious Living/Conscious Dying Project
Institute of Noetic Sciences
475 Gate Five Road, Suite 300
Sausalito, CA 94965.

- For a free copy of a Living Will write to the 50-year-old Society for the Right to Die, 250 West 57th Street, New York, NY 10107; phone (212) 246-6973.

- The address of the Hemlock Society is Box 11830, Eugene, OR 97440; phone (503) 342-5748. They offer a combination Living Will and Durable Power of Attorney plus instructions and guidance for $3 plus SASE with a .45 cent US stamp (or it comes with membership).

- Or check your local stationery store for forms.

The Institute of Noetic Sciences

is a research foundation, an educational institution, and membership organization. Founded in 1973 by Apollo 14 astronaut Edgar Mitchell, the Institute focuses on:

• **Mind-body relationships in health and healing**. We explore the connection between the mind, emotions and immune system; the phenomenon of spontaneous remission; and the unconventional new field of "energy medicine".

• **Exceptional human abilities**. We study creativity, meditation, intuitive leadership, altruism, peak performance, and "dying consciously".

• **Emerging worldviews in science and society**. We look into the relationship of consciousness and global issues, emerging paradigms in business, and "scientific causality"—the changing foundations of science in physics, biology, the neurosciences, systems theory and other fields.

We at the Institute of Noetic Sciences hold a vision of a world in which expanded human consciousness leads to a deeper understanding of untapped human potentials. We are committed to individual and institutional action which contributes to this understanding, and to the integration and practical application of the knowledge in our rapidly changing global community.

We publish books on consciousness research; the quarterly *Noetic Sciences Review,* a journal covering people and ideas in the forefront of consciousness research; *Special Reports*, which cover these ideas in more depth; and a quarterly news *Bulletin*.

For more information contact the Institute at 475 Gate Five Road, Suite 300, Sausalito, CA 94965; phone 415-331-5650.

Conscious Living/Conscious Dying Project
Statement of Purpose

The Conscious Living/Conscious Dying Project is an 18-month pilot project funded through and sponsored by the Institute of Noetic Sciences. The purpose of this project is to define and promote a better understanding of conscious dying and death in our society.

Birth and death are natural and essential components of life. Exploring the ideas and meanings of conscious death and dying has very real implications for the ways we choose to live, and the values we place upon the quality of life.

Living and dying comprise a continuum. Death is a transition, not a finality. By examining our attitudes toward one, we affect our appreciation of the other. We believe a better understanding of conscious dying—of living fully into death—will serve to encourage a healthier attitude toward death which, in turn, will enhance the quality of life for people of all ages.

For more information contact the Conscious Living/Conscious Dying Project, Institute of Noetic Sciences, at the address on page 64.

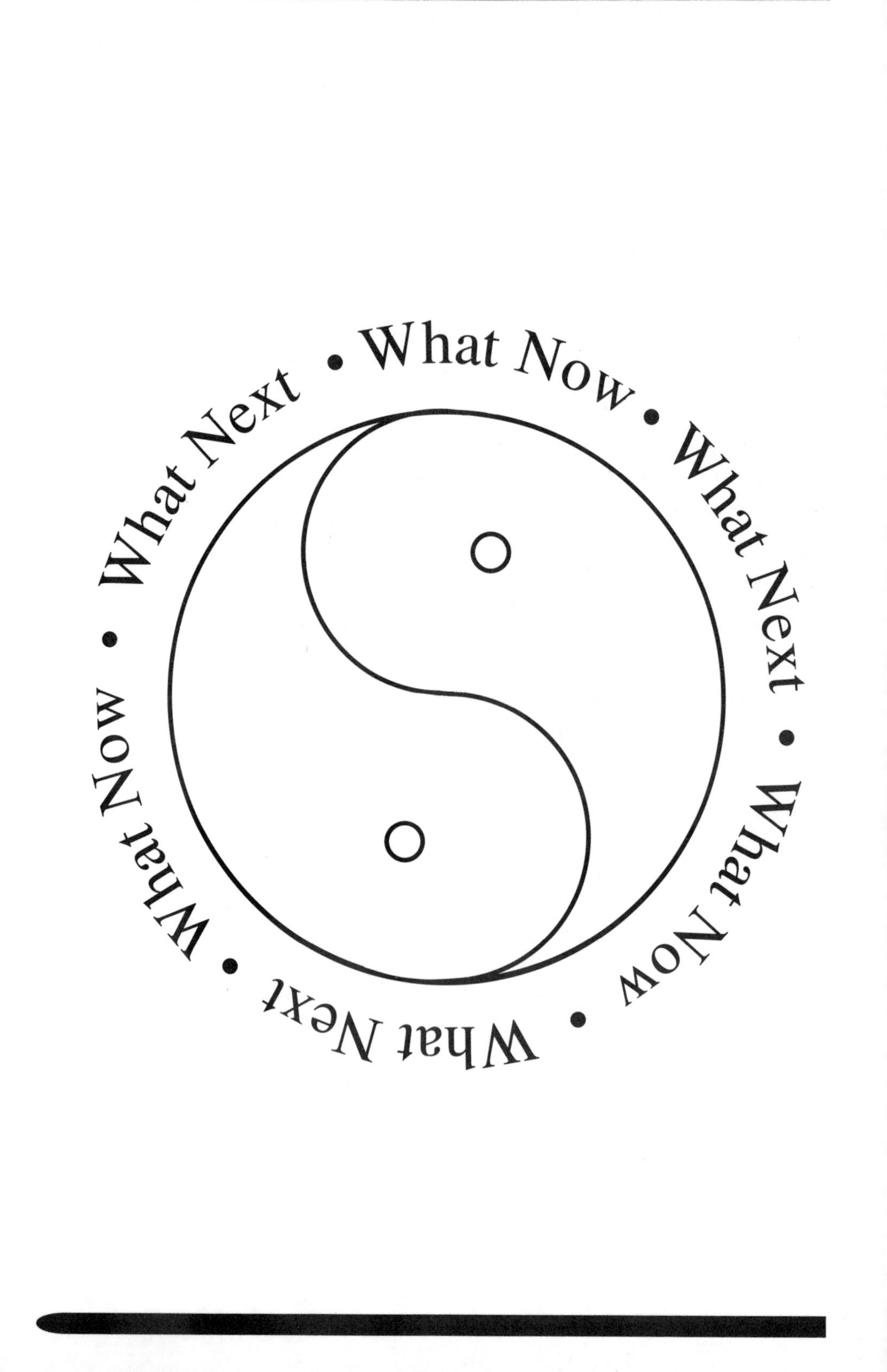
What Now • What Next • What Now • What Next • What Now • What Next • What Now • What Next •

When you were born you cried
And the whole world rejoiced.
Live such a life that when you die
The whole world cries and you rejoice.

—Traditional Indian saying

When you were born you cried
And the whole world rejoiced.
Live such a life that when you die
The whole world cries and you rejoice.

—Traditional Indian saying

A New Image of Aging

Here's a new image of aging, of becoming a whole person, in which we take responsibility for ourselves, and for reaching a balance of mind, spirit and body, by

- Developing the use of our minds
- Appreciating our wonderful bodies
- Finding our place in the universe.

And that's what we learn at Life's Finishing School.